D1283913

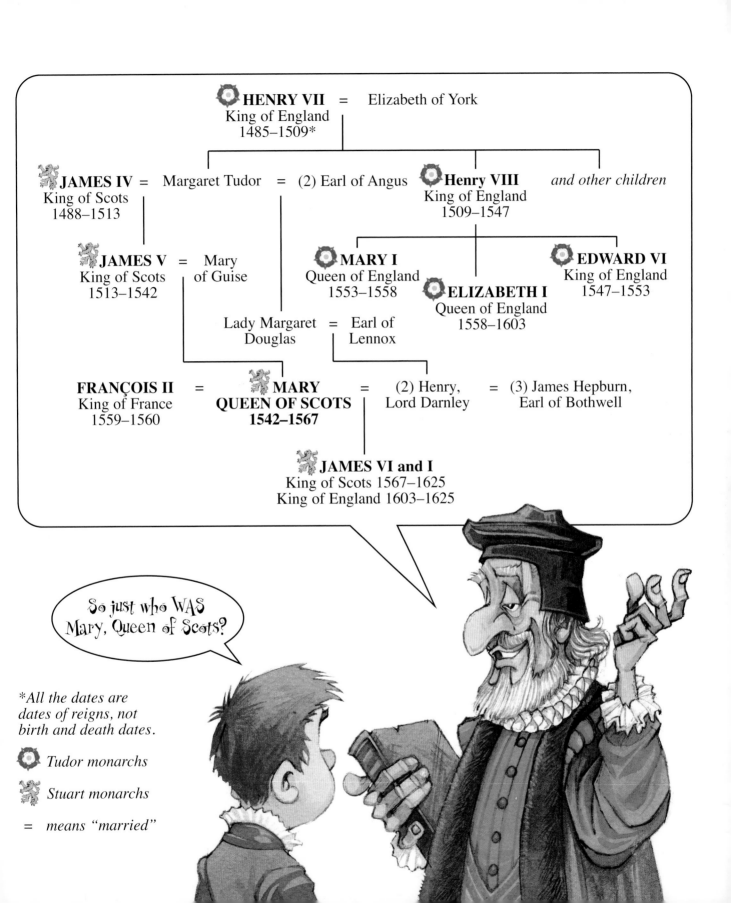

Author:
Fiona Macdonald studied history at
Cambridge University and at the University of
East Anglia, both in England. She has taught in
schools, in universities, and in adult education, and
is the author of numerous books for children on
historical topics.

Artist:
David Antram was born in Brighton, England,
in 1958. He studied at Eastbourne College of Art
and then worked in advertising for fifteen years
before becoming a full-time artist. He has
illustrated many children's nonfiction books.

Series creator:
David Salariya was born in Dundee, Scotland.
He has illustrated a wide range of books and has
created and designed many new series for
publishers in the UK and overseas. In 1989 he
established The Salariya Book Company. He lives
in Brighton, England, with his wife, illustrator
Shirley Willis, and their son Jonathan.

Editor: **Stephen Haynes**

Editorial Assistant: **Mark Williams**

© The Salariya Book Company Ltd MMVIII
No part of this publication may be reproduced in whole or in
part, or stored in a retrieval system, or transmitted in any form or
by any means, electronic, mechanical, photocopying, recording,
or otherwise, without written permission of the publisher. For
information regarding permission, write to Scholastic Inc.,
557 Broadway, New York, NY 10012.

Published in Great Britain in 2008 by
The Salariya Book Company Ltd
25 Marlborough Place, Brighton BN1 1UB

ISBN-13: 978-0-531-13912-7 (lib. bdg.) 978-0-531-14853-2 (pbk.)
ISBN-10: 0-531-13912-3 (lib. bdg.)   0-531-14853-X (pbk.)

All rights reserved.
Published in 2008 in the United States
by Franklin Watts
An imprint of Scholastic Inc.
Published simultaneously in Canada.

A CIP catalog record for this book is available
from the Library of Congress.

Printed and bound in China.
Printed on paper from sustainable sources.

You Wouldn't Want to Be
Mary, Queen of Scots!

Written by
Fiona Macdonald

Illustrated by
David Antram

Created and designed by
David Salariya

A Ruler Who Really Lost Her Head

Franklin Watts

An Imprint of Scholastic Inc.

NEW YORK • TORONTO • LONDON • AUCKLAND • SYDNEY

MEXICO CITY • NEW DELHI • HONG KONG

DANBURY, CONNECTICUT

Contents

Introduction

Your story starts on December 14, 1542. You're only days old, and you're already Queen of Scotland. As a royal ruler, a life of privilege and luxury awaits you. But so do scandals, dramas, dangers, difficult duties—and the chance of a dreadful death.

Your father, King James V, has just died. Your mother, Mary of Guise, cannot help you much. She's still weak after giving birth to you—and she's a long way from her homeland, France, and her powerful family.

Scotland, your kingdom, is poor, defenseless, and divided. Some say it is wild and uncivilized. It's certainly hard to govern! Scottish nobles, royal advisers, and religious leaders can't be trusted—they're all ambitious and greedy for power. There are rumors of plots, and your mother is struggling to keep control of the kingdom—and keep you alive.

Worst of all, you're a GIRL. In the sixteenth century, female rulers mean trouble. So, would you really want to be Mary, Queen of Scots?

SCOTLAND

Edinburgh

ENGLAND

London

FRANCE

Paris

Baby Queen: 1543-1547

Terrible Times

1541: Before you are born, your father and mother have two sons, James and Robert. Tragically, both die.

1542: Your father James V dies after being defeated by the English at Solway Moss.

1543: English soldiers attack Scotland's capital, Edinburgh, and burn Scottish villages.

1547: Scotland's best soldiers are slaughtered by the English at the Battle of Pinkie Cleugh.

ou come from two proud families: the Stuarts (or Stewarts), who rule Scotland, and the Guises, who are important nobles in France. You are also closely related to the Tudor dynasty of England. The Tudor king, mighty Henry VIII, is your great-uncle. But despite your royal heritage, you cannot pass laws, raise taxes, fight wars, or lead your people. You cannot rule at all, because you are only a baby! How can you end the fighting between rival nobles in Scotland, or the quarrels between Scottish Catholics and Protestants? And Henry VIII is launching an invasion against Scotland right now! He wants to conquer Scotland and promise you in marriage to his son, Prince Edward.

1546: Protestant leader George Wishart is burned alive by Catholics. Catholic leader Cardinal Beaton is hanged by Protestants.

1547: Protestant preacher John Knox is captured by the French and forced to row in a galley.

Escape to France

It's 1548, and Scotland is a very dangerous place. English raids across the border cause daily bloodshed, and civil war is brewing.

For safety, your mother has decided to send you to France. She has arranged for you to marry there, both for your own protection and to link Scotland with France. She promises life will be better there—but how will you cope in a foreign land? You're only five years old and don't speak French. Will you even like this French prince you must marry?

YOUR MOTHER chooses a governess and four girls (known as the "Four Marys" because they are all named Mary!) to travel with you as companions.

At Dumbarton, you board a fragile wooden ship. The winds are strong and the waves are wild—your companions are horribly seasick. When at last you reach France, you're "a poor-looking lot."

SCOTLAND
Dumbarton

ENGLAND

Roscoff   FRANCE

Wave Goodbye to:

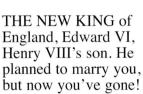

YOUR SAD, wise, and worried mother. You won't see her again for years.

SCOTTISH NOBLES and church leaders. They're still arguing over who should rule, and about Scottish religion.

THE NEW KING of England, Edward VI, Henry VIII's son. He planned to marry you, but now you've gone!

Triple Tragedy

Happy Days...

YOU'RE CLEVER and pretty; everyone admires you. King Henri calls you "the most perfect child."

YOU LIVE in beautiful palaces, with lovely gardens, pools, and fountains.

Your mother was right! You love living in France, where her family welcomes you warmly. You even make friends with gruff King Henri II and become his favorite. You spend your days very pleasantly, reading, writing, studying foreign languages—and having fun. You even grow fond of Prince François, your husband-to-be. The Prince is sickly, but devoted to you. You marry him in 1558, when you are 15.

But tragedy strikes! Your happy life is shattered when your dear father-in-law Henri II is killed. Your new husband becomes King François II, and you are now Queen of France–and Queen of Scots. But just a few months later, François dies too. So does your mother, far away in Scotland. You have seen her only once since you left. You're sad, miserable, and terribly lonely. What will happen to you now?

You make friends with the French royal children and your cousins from the Guise family.

You learn to dance and play music. They are your passions—and you're very good at both.

You wear wonderful clothes of silk and velvet, trimmed with gold and jewels.

You're happy to marry Prince François, though he's childish, grumpy, and ill. You have a splendid, fairy-tale wedding.

...Then Disaster!

1559: King Henri II fights in a tournament, just for fun. By accident, a wooden lance pierces his eye. The royal doctors cannot save him.

Handy Hint

Don't wear white for your wedding dress—it's the color of mourning in France, and is bound to bring bad luck!

1560: Your husband, the new King François II, dies when an ear infection spreads to his brain.

My, my—she should never have married in white!

11

All Alone

You're 18 years old, already a widow, and no longer Queen of France. You're charming and extremely beautiful—tall and slim, with auburn hair and hazel eyes—but you haven't produced any royal children, and you don't seem wise enough to play any part in politics. The new French king, Charles IX, sends you home.

You're still Queen of Scots, but when you return to Scotland in 1561, trouble awaits. Many Scottish people distrust your foreign French ways, and Protestants don't want you—a Catholic—as their queen. You turn for help to your half brother, the Earl of Moray. He's strong, tough, and clever, but the law bans him from ruling. Be careful—he's hungry for power!

YOUR PASTIMES include golf, falconry, hunting, and parties with your cousin Henry Darnley and other nobles. You love having fun, but are you neglecting your royal duties?

Dangers Threaten:

JOHN KNOX, now freed from the galleys, wants all women rulers to be banned.

Handy Hint

Don't get too close to Darnley! He's a great grandson of Henry VII and could be in line for the English throne. Elizabeth I, the new Queen of England, may think you are plotting against her.

SCOTTISH PROTESTANTS riot against your Catholic beliefs.

HIGHLANDERS— proud, independent people from the north of Scotland— plot to kidnap you.

That's all there is, Ma'am!

YOU HAVE no soldiers to guard you...

...and no money!

Foolish Marriage

As queen of Scotland, it's your duty to marry and produce a son and heir. If you choose to wed a Scottish noble, the others may become your enemies. But marrying a foreign prince could lead to Scotland being taken over by a stronger, rival nation. So what do you do? Foolishly, you fall madly in love with your cousin Darnley, and in 1565 you marry him. He's tall, handsome, well-dressed, and a Catholic like you—but he's also weak and selfish.

When you become pregnant, Queen Elizabeth is furious—thanks to Darnley's royal Tudor blood, your child will be the heir to the English throne!

Husband Trouble

DARNLEY'S A DISASTER! You soon find out he doesn't love you. He sulks and ignores you. He meddles in government business—and offends both Catholics and Protestants.

Stop your squawking'!

Help! Murder!

Rizzio

Don't worry, missus—it's him we're after.

Murder Mystery

After seeing Rizzio killed, you hate Darnley, but you can't divorce him now. You're expecting his baby, and any scandal would be bad for the child's future. So you are polite to Darnley in public. But you are delighted when you meet James Hepburn, Earl of Bothwell, again. You got to know him in France. He's a soldier—proud, daring, and strong. You really admire him!

At last, your baby son, James, is born. Congratulations! Now you tell your half brother, the Earl of Moray, that you're ready to divorce Darnley. Muttering mysteriously, he goes off to have secret talks with Bothwell. Soon afterwards, a massive explosion shatters Darnley's Edinburgh house. Darnley is dead!

The explosion takes place at 2 A.M. on Monday, February 10, 1567.

DARNLEY'S DEATH was meant to look like an accident, but everyone knows that he was murdered—and many people blame you!

I don't know what to do!

Mary, Queen of Scots

I'm getting out of here for a while!

Moray

Nothing to do with me!

Bothwell

Goodness! Another plot!

Scottish citizens

So far, so good!

Kidnapped!

Bothwell is accused of murdering Darnley, but his judges say he's not guilty. Not surprisingly, this makes the Scottish people very angry with you. As queen, you're responsible for upholding the law, and it's your royal duty to see that Darnley's killers are punished. Even if Bothwell isn't guilty—and he probably is—he's bound to know who did it.

But no! You continue to treat Bothwell as your friend. You even agree to meet him one fine night on your way back from seeing your son. What happens next horrifies you, but you've been warned—you know what Bothwell is like! He rides up and surrounds you with soldiers. He carries you off to Dunbar Castle and forces you to marry him.

Whoa there!

What Happens Next?

YOU THOUGHT Bothwell cared for you. Now you feel betrayed! Your wedding is miserable, and your life with Bothwell is even worse...

And another thing...

BOTHWELL IS A BRUTE, and bullies you. You cry most of the time. Other Scottish nobles are furious, and lead their soldiers to attack him.

x

18

Handy Hint

Don't listen to what people are saying about you. Some say you planned to run away with Bothwell— your husband's murderer!

BOTHWELL RIDES OFF, and you never see him again. Then you find you are pregnant with twins. What will happen to them?

THERE ARE RIOTS in Edinburgh. The Scottish people no longer want you as queen. Meanwhile, Bothwell has escaped to Denmark. But he is flung into prison by the Danish king, who knows that Bothwell is a murder suspect. He will spend the last ten years of his life there, in dreadful conditions.

I only came here because I thought I'd be safe...

Queen No More

You're locked up again, this time in Lochleven Castle north of Edinburgh. You've been put there by your half brother, the Earl of Moray, and other Scottish nobles. They're furious with Bothwell for marrying you without telling them. They say that you've been foolish, as well as a danger to Scotland. They demand that you abdicate (give up the throne). So in July 1567 your baby son James is crowned as Scotland's new king—James VI.

IN THE DARK, damp castle you become very ill. Your twins— Bothwell's children—both die.

Admit it!

MORAY ACCUSES YOU of helping Bothwell kill Darnley. He knows you are innocent, but he wants you to stay locked up.

HIS PLAN FAILS. One of your guards, George Douglas, falls deeply in love with you.

Handy Hint

Don't imagine you'll be welcome in England. Queen Elizabeth doesn't want you there—she's sure you'll cause trouble.

What? Does she think I haven't got problems enough of my own?

YOU SIGN AWAY all your powers as queen. You fear that you'll be killed if you refuse.

MORAY BECOMES REGENT—caretaker ruler on behalf of baby James. He takes away your jewels, saying they belong to the nation—but keeps some for himself.

Goodbye to Scotland

DOUGLAS IS KIND, gentle, romantic. He becomes your faithful servant and stays with you for many years. He helps you to disguise yourself as a servant, find a boat, and escape from the castle across the lake.

TOGETHER, you and Douglas ride wildly toward England. This time, the Scottish people are behind you. With the hated Bothwell gone, some of the nobles also hurry to support you. But Moray is waiting for you, with soldiers!

DEFEAT. You and your followers fight at Langside near Glasgow but are defeated. You and Douglas are forced to flee for your lives. At last you reach the border.

In Prison—On Trial

A boatman rows you across the river. At last you reach England. You're expecting your cousin Elizabeth to offer you comfort and shelter. But, to your horror, she treats you with suspicion, as a rival for her throne. She fears you will stir up the Catholic rebels against her and her Protestant faith.

For Elizabeth, you're a real problem. She wishes you would go away. There's no room in England for another royal ruler! Elizabeth can't execute you—that would be wrong—so she puts you in prison. She claims this is for your own protection, but really she wants to hide you away and end your political power.

So sad! So lovely!

Poor wee thing!

Who's Pleased to See You in England?

ELIZABETH FEARS that many English people will want you, not her, as their queen. You are far more gracious and appealing!

So tragic!

She shares our faith.

Your first jailers

Politically, a useful ally!

Charming!

People who pity your unhappy life

Catholics

Ambassadors from Catholic France, Italy, and Spain

The letters prove it!

They're mostly fakes, but who's to know?

Handy Hint

Take up a hobby to pass the time in prison. You like sewing, so why not embroider a bedspread or some curtains?

The "Casket Letters"

THE ENGLISH claim that you knew Bothwell was going to kill Darnley—and they say they have letters from you to prove it! You know you are innocent, but will anyone believe you?

Who's Not?

Wrong beliefs!

A threat!

We don't need her sort here!

A nuisance!

OTHER ENGLISH PEOPLE are not so excited to see you. They fear you might provoke quarrels, or even cause a civil war. They're not impressed by the way you ruled Scotland. They'd be happy to see you in prison forever!

English Protestants

Government officials

Queen Elizabeth's friends

Long-term jailers

23

Stop Plotting!

For a person like you who loves sports and dancing, it's misery to be locked away. Day by day, you see your life slowly passing you by. You hope and pray that Queen Elizabeth will soon let you out of prison. But, foolishly, while you wait, you take part in plotting against her.

Of course you hate being a prisoner—but you're becoming far too dangerous to be let out. Over the years, many people die for trying to plot your escape. Many of them are tortured and executed in horrible ways. So stop and think before you plot!

1569–1570: Nobles from the north of England rebel against Elizabeth. They want to bring back the Catholic faith, and they want you as their Catholic queen. The rebellion fails, and they die.

1581: Queen Elizabeth passes strict new laws to ban Catholic worship in England. She wants to keep tight control over you and your Catholic supporters.

RIDOLFI PLOT, 1571: The Pope sends spies to England, hoping to overthrow Elizabeth with the help of the Spanish and then set you free. The plot is discovered and the plotters are executed.

I wonder, is anyone trying to set me free right now?

Handy Hint

Don't put your plans in writing! Queen Elizabeth's spies are lurking everywhere!

¡Adiós!

THROCKMORTON PLOT, 1583: Spain plans to invade and make you queen. The plot is discovered and the Spanish ambassador is expelled.

GIFFORD PLOT, 1585: You smuggle out letters to Catholic friends who want you set free. The letters are found and your friends are executed.

25

All Over...

It's 1587, and you've been a prisoner for almost 20 years. You're weak and depressed, and Queen Elizabeth has been busy taking power away from you. She's even persuaded your son, King James VI of Scotland, to ban you from ruling there.

Now Elizabeth has learned of yet another plot against her—the so-called Babington Plot. This time she has proof that you were part of it. It's the last straw—now you will lose your head!

You go so graciously to your death that all who watch are in tears. After heartfelt prayers, you kneel, the ax falls…

…and it's all over.

Dying in Style

WEAR A BLOOD-RED DRESS. It's the color of Catholic martyrs. This will show everyone that, although you may have made mistakes, you trust God will forgive you.

KEEP YOUR WIG ON! In prison, your stunning auburn hair has grown thin and pale. So you wear a wig to remind everyone you were once Europe's most glamorous queen.

Fotheringay Castle, Northamptonshire, England: February 8, 1587

Handy Hint

Don't give up! Choose a motto that looks beyond death to a glorious future.

In my end is my beginning.

KEEP SMILING! All your life you've looked lovely, and you die beautifully, too. A wax death mask will record your face, finally at peace. In this way your image will be preserved for hundreds of years.

DON'T GO ALONE. Your little pet dogs like to hide under your skirts. They stay there, whimpering and wriggling, even after you're dead.

Not Forgotten

Your death was welcomed by many in England and Scotland. It solved so many problems! Your reign is remembered as a troubled time, made worse by your mistakes and weaknesses. Yet your royal heritage survives—triumphantly! When Queen Elizabeth dies in 1603, your son James becomes King of England, founding a new Stuart dynasty there. The Stuarts rule Britain until 1714 and marry into royal and noble families throughout Europe. Today, many famous people—including the present Queen of the United Kingdom, Elizabeth II—are descended from you.

Queen Elizabeth I had no children. But just look who's descended from me!

TURN TO PAGE 31
to find out more about
Mary's descendants.

James the First and Sixth,* that's me—King of England **and** Scotland.

*James I of England,
James VI of Scotland.

Handy Hint

See for yourself how you are still remembered in countless books for children and adults, and on the World Wide Web.

How Else Will You Be Remembered?

AS A VICTIM to be pitied: teenage widow, lonely queen, deserted wife. As a beautiful romantic, who sought love but found suffering. As a loyal Catholic, a Scottish heroine, and an unfortunate but fascinating woman.

TODAY, you're buried in a splendid tomb close to Queen Elizabeth I, your old enemy. Alive, you never met; Elizabeth felt too angry. But now you're together for all eternity.

Glossary

Abdicate To give up being queen or king.

Casket A small box for storing valuable items. The "Casket Letters" are a group of eight letters and some poems that are supposed to have been written by Mary, Queen of Scots. They were found in a silver casket belonging to her. Mary's enemies used the letters to "prove" that she had had Lord Darnley murdered, but many historians believe that parts of the letters were faked.

Death mask A wax or plaster cast of a person's face made immediately after that person's death.

Falconry A form of hunting, using specially trained hawks or falcons to hunt other birds or small mammals.

Galley A ship driven by oars as well as sails. Prisoners were often forced to row in galleys as a punishment.

Heir The person next in line to be king or queen.

Martyr A person who is willing to die for their religion.

Regent A person who rules on behalf of a king or queen because the king or queen is too young or too ill to rule.

Scot A Scottish person. The official title of the Scottish monarch was King or Queen of Scots—not of Scotland.

Scots A dialect (regional variety) of English that is spoken in Scotland—not to be confused with Scots Gaelic, which is an entirely different language.

Tournament A sporting contest that included mock battles.

The Stuart Dynasty

There were nine Stuart rulers of Scotland:

Robert II	reigned	1371–1390
Robert III		1390–1406
James I		1406–1437
James II		1437–1460
James III		1460–1488
James IV		1488–1513
James V		1513–1542
Mary		**1542–1567**
James VI		1567–1625

In 1603, James VI of Scotland also became James I of England. After him, there were five more Stuart rulers of England and Scotland:

Charles I	reigned	1625–1649
Charles II		1660–1685*
James II		1685–1688
Mary II		1689–1694**
Anne		1702–1714

In 1707, during Queen Anne's reign, England and Scotland were united to become Great Britain. Queen Anne had no surviving children. She was followed by George I, the first of the Hanoverian dynasty. He was descended from James I's eldest daughter, Princess Elizabeth. All later kings and queens of Great Britain (and of the United Kingdom, formed in 1800) are therefore descended from James I and VI, the son of Mary, Queen of Scots.

There was no monarch during the Civil War and Commonwealth period, 1649–1660.
**Mary's husband, William III, ruled with her, and continued until he died in 1702.

Index